Customer Service 201:

Managing Your People To Be Their Best

Renée Evenson

Bull'sEye
PUBLISHING

To my husband Joe,
whose support and encouragement
helped me complete this project.

To my daughter Michelle,
who is just starting out in the business world.

And to Stephanie Ward of TeleSet,
who helped me achieve my goal.

Publisher's Note: Additional copies of this manual are available for purchase. Other manuals in this series, posters, introductory packages and special prices for quantity purchases are also available. We are consistently updating and introducing new series. Please contact Bull'sEye Publishing at the address and phone listed below.

Customer Service 201: *Managing Your People To Be Their Best*

Copyright © 1997 Renée Evenson

Library of Congress Catalog Card No.: 96-95313

ISBN 1-890181-01-3

PO Box 599 • Whitehouse Station, NJ 08889 • (908) 534-8728

PRINTED IN THE UNITED STATES OF AMERICA.

Introduction

I n today's marketplace, with so much competition for a customer's business, the only edge you may have is in the way you treat your customers. It is a fact that consumers will pay more, drive farther and inconvenience themselves to do business with a company that treats them well. Providing consistently good service is an important factor of success in any business. Providing exceptional customer service will build the bond that will keep your customers coming back time and time again because you treat them better than your competition.

Why do customers take their business elsewhere?
Some move away. Some change because they are not satisfied with the product. Some go because of competitive reasons. But the majority of customers take their business elsewhere because of an indifferent attitude toward them by the owner, manager, or an employee. Most of the time, these customers will not even complain. They just will not come back.

Can you afford to give less than your best when serving your customers?

Not if you want to be your customer's number one choice!

Learn and follow the tips in this book and you will be your best at what you do, so you can help your employees be their best at what they do.

Being your best will bring you self-satisfaction, confidence in your abilities, devoted employees and loyal customers — friends for life.

The Platinum Rule

G iving good customer service is nothing more than observing the Golden Rule. Treat your customers the way you want to be treated as a customer. Giving exceptional customer service means going the extra mile by following the Golden Rule with enthusiasm and creativity. That is the Platinum Rule.

Customer Service 101 Revisited

How familiar are you with the lessons in *Customer Service 101?* You must first learn and follow all the lessons in the book before you can expect your employees to do likewise. The best way to show your employees what you have learned is by demonstrating those same lessons.

Just as your employees interact with customers in their job, your employees are *your* customers. Deal with your employees the same way you expect them to deal with their customers. Follow the Platinum Rule with your employees and it will be easier for them to follow it with their customers.

Just handing the book to your employees will work only for those who are self-motivated enough to take the initiative to read it on their own. Most likely, those are your most valued employees, or translated, the ones who already innately follow the majority of the lessons.

For those employees, give them the book, but be sure to let them know how much you appreciate the terrific job they are doing in handling customers. Tell them you would like their feedback on what lessons they find most beneficial after they read the book. Pick out one or two that they do particularly well, and point out that you have observed them already using those lessons.

For the employees who need the book the most, you will need to invest a great deal of time initially. And be prepared to do some follow-up observations to insure they have learned the valuable tips. Set aside time to meet individually with each employee to jointly work through the book. You will most likely want to work one chapter at a time, or in some cases, one lesson at a time.

Before the first meeting, give the employee the book, then tell him you will meet with him (date and time) to begin working through it, one segment at a time. Ask the employee to look through the book and select the chapter or the lesson he would like to work on first.

When you meet for your first training session, ask the employee what segment he selected and why. It is important that the employee make the decision on the lesson in which he feels he needs the most help. He will place more emphasis on learning the material if he makes the choice about what he wants to learn. Unless there is a drastic problem that needs to be fixed immediately, it is OK if you do not agree with his decision. Besides, you will cover all the chapters, anyway.

Asking the employee up front why he chose a particular chapter will get him to respond about a problem he may be having. Or it may be that he is merely uncomfortable in a certain area. Depending on the employee and his response, you may decide to break down the chapter and work lesson by lesson. You will be the judge of what will work best based on where the employee is.

Read through the chapter or the lesson together. Be prepared to role play a contact where you play the customer. Tell the employee to keep the book open as you role play so he can refer back to the tip or tips he is trying to improve.

Your employee may stumble and not be able to think of the right response. Give him time to come up with a solution on his own, but do not let him stumble too long. It is all right to help him. After all, this is a training session. Work together to come up with a good response.

Set up your next training session, but be sure to tell your employee you appreciated his input during this meeting. Let him know you will be available if he needs any help with what he just learned. Assure him you know he will do a good job. Then try to observe your employee utilizing the lesson with a customer. Be sure to offer your positive and constructive thoughts.

If the employee is having a severe problem in one of the areas, of course you will want to work on that section, first. In this case, you will not even ask the employee to choose a chapter. Your discussion of the problem will be your focal point for introducing the book to the employee.

Without getting offensive, tell the employee you have observed some contacts in that particular area. Tell him that you think learning a different approach would be more helpful in his interactions with customers.

You will want to read through the chapter or the lesson with the employee. Have some previously observed examples prepared for the discussion. After reading, you might say something like this:

"Joe, remember your contact with Mrs. Brown last week? She was upset that her order hadn't been delivered and took it out on you? Remember how you came back at her by saying that maybe we tried to make a delivery and perhaps she wasn't home? She flew off the handle and got really angry when you said that. Looking through the section we just read on dealing with difficult customers, how could you have handled the contact with her differently?"

In this example, you focused on the contact — or problem — not on the employee. You stressed the behavior without judging.

Hopefully, Joe will respond with something like:
"Well, rather than telling her that maybe we tried delivering and she wasn't home, I could have apologized, and maybe even said something like I know that waiting for something can be pretty frustrating. Then I could have told her that usually the orders take two weeks to deliver. And I could have offered to check on the order to see if it had been shipped out."
"That's sounds good. You apologized and displayed empathy by showing your understanding for the frustration she was feeling. Then you gave her additional information about our turn-around time and even went one step further by offering to check on the order for her. How do you think she would have responded?"
Now be quiet and let Joe talk. Most managers do not know when to shut up and let the employee do the talking. And in a case like this, Joe will most likely judge his own actions.
"She probably would have hung up happy that I was going to check her order instead of banging the phone down. You know, she really got to me when she came on the line. I guess I took it personally. And now that we went through this, I can see that my getting defensive only added fuel to her fire. Next time, I'll try to follow the

advice in the book about not getting defensive. I think that is my biggest problem with customers. I'll try to remember they aren't mad at me, personally."

Now you will reinforce Joe that you know he can do just that. The best part about this approach is that Joe was the one who recognized his own problem.

Not every employee will accept responsibility as easily as Joe did, and not every employee is going to get whatever it is you are trying to teach the first time. The idea is to focus on the problem, focus on the employee's behavior, let the employee find the solution in the book, and then role play the situation handled in a better way. Believe me, this works. Just do not become frustrated if you don't succeed the first time. After all, this is new to many of you, too.

Taking the necessary time to train your employees on the art of dealing with customers in a positive manner will more than pay off in the dividends you will receive. Those dividends will be in the form of observing your employees using the Platinum Rule. Eventually you will see them doing it naturally. They will feel better about themselves, and you can take pride in knowing that you helped develop your employees to be their best.

If you have an employee who does not respond to the lessons in this book, you will need to help the employee see that he is in the wrong line of work. It is your responsibility to invest the time in training your employees to do it the right way. It is not your responsibility to continue to pay an employee who chooses to do it the wrong way.

Customer Service 101 Revisited
~ *Thoughts & Ideas* ~

Customer Service 101 Revisited

My Personal Planner

Contents

Chapter 1

Think Leadership

A re you enthusiastically committed to your company's mission and goals? Do you take responsibility for your actions? Are you open, honest, and trustworthy? Are you flexible and adaptive? Do you welcome change? Do you genuinely care about your customers? Do you genuinely care about your company results? Are you a team player? Do you know how to lead? Do you know how to follow? Are you skilled and sensitive when dealing with people? Are you constantly looking for ways to improve, to learn?

Did you answer yes to all of the questions? If you did, you are a true leader. If you answered no to some, don't worry, you, like most managers, have some skills to master. If you answered no to most, or all, it's time to worry. You are either in the wrong line of work, or have a lot of skills to master. You need to assess your strengths and weaknesses. You need to decide if you are committed to improving your skills. You need to know if you want to be a leader.

Be consistent with your team.
People want to know they can expect the same treatment
from their boss day after day.

It is more important
that your people respect you than like you.

Be a positive role model.

Always use appropriate language and grammar.

Earn your employees' trust.
Be honest and up front with them.

Honesty will build trust,
which will build loyalty, which will bring success.

Treat everyone as though
they are equally important to you.

Do not act as if you are above doing any job.

———————————

Share your success with your team,
but take responsibility for blame.

———————————

Be responsible for you own attitude.

———————————

Do not wait around for someone else to make the decisions.

———————————

One of the most important traits you can possess is resiliency.

———————————

Act positive,
and you will begin to feel positive.

———————————

Stick with the basics.

═══════════

Think Leadership
~ *Thoughts & Ideas* ~

Think Leadership

My leadership strengths are:

My leadership areas of improvement are:

Chapter 2

Company Mission, Goals And Measurements

Would you ever pack your car for a vacation and take off with your family, not knowing your destination? Let's suppose you did just that. You decided to pack a road map so you would have some sense of direction. You have everything you need — you are ready to go. You and your family leave. You are blindly following the map, but how will you know when you get "there" when you never decided where "there" was? You would probably come home exhausted, having spent so much valuable time not knowing where you were headed and not knowing if you ever got there. You would not have a very successful or fulfilling vacation this way.

Running a company without a mission or goals would have the same effect.

Does your company have a mission statement? A mission statement tells in very exact words what your company stands for; what your aim is. It is your destination.

Having a mission statement provides everyone in your organization with a sole focus. Everything you do in your job should in some way relate to your company mission. Make sure yours tells very specifically what your company aim truly is. Include a statement about your customers.

A mission statement should not be very long.

Analyze what your company stands for.
What service or product do you provide?
What level of performance do you expect?
How do you expect your customers to be treated?

Your mission statement might be something like:
Our mission is to be our customer's provider of choice for _____; by offering high quality and reasonably priced products; by looking for new and innovative ways to improve; by achieving superior performance; and by demonstrating our care and concern for our customers by focusing on their needs.

Once you know specifically what your mission is, or what you are aiming for, the only way for you to reach that destination is by setting company goals. Short and long term goals are your road map to reach your target.

Once you have set your goals, or you think you are headed in the right direction, the only way you will know whether you are on the right road is by measuring your achievements.

If you are a manager of a company, it is very effective to form a mission statement for your team. It should be a modified version of your company's mission, and in fact, it should sound quite similar.

Focus on your company's mission daily.

———————

Live up to your company's mission and values.

———————

Teach your employees your company mission statement.
Make sure they understand it.

———————

Set goals.
Clearly communicate those goals to your employees
so they have a sense of direction.

———————

Set only goals
that will move you towards your mission.

———————

Help your employees set goals for themselves.

Have team meetings
on a regular basis
to share company goals.
Use this meeting time to recognize achievements
in customer service and other result areas.

Make sure you have a written job description
of all tasks you expect your employee to perform.
Review it with the employee
and provide her with a copy.
Ask questions to make sure
you have a common understanding.

Include in the job description
what the task is,
how it is to be done and
why it is done.

Review the job responsibilities of your employees,
and update when needed.
As a part of their routine,
do they do busy work
that contributes little value?

Establish a clear vision
of the quality of customer service you expect.

Communicate that vision to your employees.

Make sure that level of service
is important to your employees.

———————

Why measure?

It brings focus to achieving company goals.

It shows how effective you are.

It helps in setting goals and
monitoring trends.

It identifies input for analyzing problem areas.

It gives employees a sense of accomplishment.

It helps you monitor progress.

———————

Do you measure your customer service
based on what *you* think
your customers want?

How can you measure
the level of service you are providing?

Why not ask your customers
how well you are performing?

Have a customer response system in place,
whether it be comment cards,
random mail-outs, or handled by follow-up calls.
Let your customers tell you
how well you are doing in the service area.

Ask your customers how well
are you meeting their needs,
how can you improve,
what do they like best about your company,
and what are you not doing
that they would like you to do.

———————————

When you receive measurement data
from your customers,
post the results in a place visible to all employees.
Use the results to improve or celebrate.

———————————

Company Mission, Goals And Measurements
~ Thoughts & Ideas ~

Company Mission, Goals And Measurements

My mission is:

My goals are:

Chapter 3

Communication

Y ou need to communicate to your employees how you expect them to treat your customers. The commitment to providing exceptional customer service must be communicated from the top down. Your employees look to you to set the level of expectation. And unless you expect a certain level of performance you will not get it. You *can never* expect your employees to give more than you are willing to give. You *can* expect your employees to give what you are willing to accept.

The best way to communicate with your people
is to be with them.

———————————

Being patient
is also a part of communication.

———————————

Do you finish other people's sentences for them?
Don't.

———————————

Be interested in your people.

———————————

Ask questions to gain understanding.
It always helps to understand why someone does something.

———————————

The more you talk, the less you listen.

———————————

Are you only hearing what is being said?
Look for what is really being communicated.

———————————

Look people in the eye when communicating with them.

Keep your employees updated
on what is going on in your company.

———————————

Always pay attention to body language.
That includes yours.

———————————

Listen to your employees,
understand them,
and respond to them.

———————————

Ask, rather than tell.

———————————

Help your employees understand WHY
you are asking them to do something.
They may not always agree,
but if they understand the reason,
you are more likely to gain acceptance.

———————————

Be sure you are approachable to your employees.

The first item on your meeting agenda
should always be *Customer Service.*

Use "we" rather than "I" whenever possible.

Communication
~ Thoughts & Ideas ~

Communication

My communication strengths are:

My communication areas of improvement are:

Chapter 4

Creativity, Innovation And Efficiency

All customers have needs. Just meeting the customers' needs will not win loyalty. Customers also have expectations. They will measure your company not by how well you have met their needs, but rather by how well you have exceeded their expectations. You must continuously look for innovative and creative ways to improve, to build a customer link for life. In doing so, you must continue to maintain a high level of efficiency. Customers will not stay loyal if you sacrifice efficiency for the sake of being creative and innovative.

Performance that was outstanding yesterday
will be only mediocre today,
and inadequate tomorrow.
Strive to improve every day.

———————————

Be on the lookout
for areas that need to be improved or changed.

———————————

Be careful not to make changes
where none are needed.

———————————

Discuss areas for improvement with employees.

———————————

When possible,
let employees share in decision making.

———————————

Ask for their opinions.

Make your employees feel valued;
make them feel their input counts.

And make sure their input *does* count to you.

———————————

Let your employees be creative.
You will have to learn to let go and give people
the chance to do it their way.

Yes, mistakes will be made.

But they will learn from those mistakes.

———————————

Allowing employees to share in some decisions
will make it easier for them to accept the decisions
you are not able to let them share.

———————————

When implementing a new procedure,
anticipate problems
and discuss them with your employees
before they occur.

Do not just talk about problems; solve them.

You can always rely on
your common sense and good judgment
to solve any problem.

When you have a problem,
talk it over with your employees.
Ask for their input and suggestions.

The steps to solving a problem are:

Recognize there is a problem.

Analyze the problem.

Come up with alternative solutions.

Select the best solution.

Put your plan into action.

Follow up to be sure your solution is satisfactory.

=====================

Creativity, Innovation And Efficiency
~ *Thoughts & Ideas* ~

Creativity, Innovation And Efficiency
*I demonstrate my
creativity, innovation, and efficiency by:*

*I will improve my
creativity, innovation, and efficiency by:*

Chapter 5

Customer Care
And Quality Service

W e all provide services to others, every day. We willingly do things for our families, friends, and even strangers. So it seems that providing customers with good service should come naturally to us. For most of us, it does not. Somehow, we shift our focus when we enter work and suddenly find a need to be taught how to serve others.

Your most important role as a manager is to teach your employees how to provide the level of service you and your company expect. Your role will be one of teacher, coach, model, actor, cheerleader, and maybe even psychologist when interacting with your employees as well as your customers.

The only way for you to keep your customers
is to provide the best possible service.
You must get close to your customers.
Build a strong relationship with them.

Do you really know who your customers are?
What do they do?
What are their needs?
How do you fit in with them?
What does it take to please them?
How can you make their lives easier?

What is customer service?
And who defines it?
The customer decides
what is takes to make him satisfied.
It is up to you to ask your customer what it takes.

As the manager,
never accept or tolerate
less than the best customer service
from your employees.

Everyone in your organization
is responsible for customer service.
Service does not stop with the people
who regularly talk to customers.

————————

Whether or not your employees
have a direct link with the customer,
they all have an effect on customer service.
It is very important that each of your employees
understands this link.

————————

It is very important
that all of your employees
have an understanding of what everyone else
in the organization does.
Your employees will have
more respect for each other
if they have an idea of what the other employees do.

————————

Good service can only be achieved
when each employee feels personally responsible
for satisfying each customer.

Customers appreciate the following qualities in an employee:

Courtesy

Knowledge of services and products

Reliability

Decision making ability

Availability

Do you measure your employees on these qualities?

Customers will generally remember your company
in two instances:

When the product or service is particularly poor, or

When the product or service is extremely good.

How are your customers remembering your company?

When you just *meet* your customers' requirements
you will not stand out in their minds.

Make sure your policies make it easy
for your customers to do business with you.

Be sure your employees understand
the reason for company policies
before you expect them to
uphold those policies with customers.
Your employees must be able to
explain the "why" to customers.

———————————

Treat your customers the way you expect
your employees to treat your customers.
Better yet,
treat your customers better than that.
Most likely, your employees will strive to emulate you.

———————————

Do not ever make negative comments
about your customers
to your employees.
If you do, they will treat those customers likewise.

Even if the customer deserved it!
Bite your tongue instead.

═══════════════

Customer Care And Quality Service
~ *Thoughts & Ideas* ~

Customer Care And Quality Service
My employees and I
provide our customers with quality service by:

My employees and I
will improve our customer service by:

Chapter 6

Your Interactions
With Customers

M ost likely, your employees interact with your customers
much more frequently than you do. You probably only get
to speak to the ones who are either (A) extremely elated
with the service, or (B) not happy with the service for some reason.

To speak to the (A) customer, the service will have to be so terrific,
it makes the customer want to take the time to tell you. Customers
will not bother commending an employee, service or product unless
it was way above what they expected.

You will speak to the (B) customer much more frequently. It does
not take some customers much at all to demand to speak with a manager. Other customers will wait longer, sometimes too long, until they
ask for the manager.

No matter the problem, just be glad the customer is giving you the
chance to help them.

Let's first discuss the (A) customer. Because these kinds of contacts do not happen very often, they can often leave a manager lack-
ing for the right words to say. When a customer commends an
employee, or a service, or a product:

Thank the customer for taking the time to tell you about the employee, service or product.

Write down what the customer is saying. Write down the adjectives used to describe the employee or product.

If the customer is praising an employee, let the customer know you appreciate her positive comments and you will pass it on to the employee. Also let her know that you will make a note of her contact to place in the employee's file. If the customer is praising a product or service, let the customer know that you will pass on her comments to the appropriate department.

You may also want to send a follow up letter of thanks.

Now, on to the (B) customer.

Basically, you will handle the customer using the same care and consideration that is taught in *Customer Service 101, The Difficult Customer.*

And if you train your employees the right way to handle a difficult customer, you should not have to become involved all that often.

Your employees will be capable of handling the customer to satisfaction.

It is up to you to teach your employees how valuable your customers are, and the best way to do that is to never say anything negative about them.

If an employee ridicules a difficult customer, you need to stop that kind of negative talk immediately. You can say something like, "Looking at it from the customer's perspective, I can see why he was upset."

The main lesson that will fall on your shoulders is the one about the cost of keeping a customer. Some customers will cost you a lot to satisfy them. Some of those customers will not be worth keeping. That decision will fall on your shoulders. If you decide to end a business relationship, do not put the customer down to your employees. Be up front with them. Tell them "Our company can no longer afford the cost of keeping that customer satisfied." Period. End of conversation about that customer.

Then focus on keeping the customers you can satisfy.

Your Interactions With Customers
~ *Thoughts & Ideas* ~

Your Interactions With Customers

*When a customer compliments an employee
or our company, I will:*

When a customer complains, I will:

Teamwork

hy the focus on teamwork?
Webster's definition of teamwork answers that question:

Teamwork is the cooperative effort
by the members of a group or
team to achieve a common goal.

The words "to achieve a common goal" sum up the importance of teamwork.

Without teamwork, where will you all go if you are each heading in a different direction? How will any of you know which one of you has reached the goal? And how will you know which is the right goal?

You have heard it before. Two can do it better and faster than one.

It is true. As long as the two share common goals.

Build a strong team.
You cannot do it alone.

Building a strong, self-supportive, committed team
takes a lot of your time initially;
a lot less time thereafter.

Think of yourself and your team
as the owners of your company.

What are you and your team contributing to
the overall success of your company?

Ask for feedback on your performance from your team.

Learn to delegate.
But also learn to delegate to the right people.

Know an easy way to boost the energy level of your team?

Keep a smile on your face. A genuine smile.

Be sincere.

Be involved with your team.

Build an environment of support for each other.

Keep your own energy level high.

Know a long-lasting way to boost the effectiveness of your team?

Have a strongly defined purpose with clear cut goals.

Promote participation from all members.

Respect everyone's right to have different opinions.

Have well-defined decision making procedures.

Develop open communication.

Make sure everyone knows their role and job assignment.

Share the leadership with your team.

Foster independent thinking.

Create an atmosphere of support and cooperation.

Focus on measures and areas of improvement.

Teamwork
~ Thoughts & Ideas ~

Teamwork

My coaching strengths are:

My coaching areas of improvement are:

Chapter 8

Employee Commitment
And Loyalty

N ever be afraid to expect a high level of commitment and loyalty from your employees. After all, if they do not feel committed and loyal, maybe they are in the wrong job. Just as
importantly, make sure you value their commitment and loyalty. Be
the kind of boss they respect. Respect them, first.

Be committed and loyal to your employees, first.

———————————

Never allow yourself nor your employees
to become complacent.

———————————

Ask for and act on suggestions for improvement.

———————————

Put yourself in your employee's shoes.

———————————

Let your employees know they can
count on you to be there for them.

———————————

Make your employees feel valued.

———————————

Remember to make your high-performance employees feel valued.

Tell them they are important to you.

Reward good performance
with additional responsibilities.

Help your employees to have fun in their job.

Make your employees feel good about coming to work.

Give them credit when you put
their ideas into action.

Employee Commitment And Loyalty
~ *Thoughts & Ideas* ~

Employee Commitment And Loyalty

I demonstrate my commitment and loyalty by:

I will improve my commitment and loyalty by:

Chapter 9

Continual Learning

L earning never stops. You learn something. Change comes. You must learn something new, or learn the old in a new way. Be a good learner. Also, be a good teacher. Tell, show, demonstrate, help, stand by, nudge, offer encouragement. And do not just do any of the above once. Learning, as well as teaching, is continual.

It all begins with the training process.

Do your employees know what you expect of them?
What kind of training have you provided to your employees?
You cannot expect them to do the right thing
unless they know what the right thing is.

Spend time up front
properly training your employees
to do the job you hired them to do.

Demonstrate how
you want your employees to do the job.

As a part of your training,
do you include how to use your phone equipment?
Do not assume a new employee
will know how to use the features such as hold,
transfer, and conferencing.

If you cannot answer an employee's question,
tell him you will get the answer.
Never lie.

―――――――

Everyone has different "buttons,"
different methods of learning,
different strengths and weaknesses.
Get to know your employees,
so you know the best approach
to deal with each person.

―――――――

Teach your employees about the entire organization
and how their job relates to the company.

―――――――

Spend time training your employees
on the behaviors you expect.

―――――――

Let your employees know
what you expect of them.

Change is never easy, especially for customers.
There are times when you will need to make a change,
either to a product or to a service.
Make sure your employees fully understand the change
and why it was done
before expecting them to talk to customers about it.

Do not just tell your people how wonderful the change will be.
They will accept it better
if you give them a more balanced viewpoint.
With any change, there will always be good and bad.
Discuss both.

When a change is implemented,
you will need to spend more time monitoring your employees
to insure their understanding.

Teach your employees how to solve their own problems.
Before you readily give them the answer,
ask them some leading questions
to see if they can come up with a viable solution.
Ask them "What do you think you should do?"

Continual Learning
~ *Thoughts & Ideas* ~

Continual Learning

My teaching strengths are:

My teaching areas of improvement are:

Chapter 10

Motivating To Develop
High Performers

M otivation, like learning and teaching, is a continual process. Motivation occurs when people feel good about their accomplishments. They strive to do even better. But if their accomplishments go unnoticed, if they feel no one cares, the drive to do better wanes. People want to hear a word of encouragement. They want someone to notice when they do something well, something out of the ordinary. They want to know their efforts are important. That goes for everyone. If someone tells you they do not care about hearing something positive about themselves, don't believe them. It's human nature to want to be recognized. And there is no better motivation than recognition.

Never underestimate
the power of a word of encouragement.

Or a smile, or a pat on the back,
or a thumbs up. . .

You get the idea.

Acknowledge good performance immediately.

It is OK to praise in public,
as long as you know it is OK with the employee.

It is *never* OK to reprimand in public.

Remember to offer positive feedback
to those employees who consistently do it right.
Try to give them additional responsibilities
so they may continue to grow.

Recognize and reward
customer service accomplishments,
both individually and total team efforts.

Some ways to recognize your employee's successes:

Recognition —
do it in a meeting, post it on a board,
give the employee a special parking spot for a designated period;

Award —
it does not have to be something extravagant,
just a token of your appreciation;
take the employee to lunch,
buy a box of candy, give a movie gift certificate;

Compensation —
again, it does not have to be extravagant —
an hour off with pay, an extended lunch hour,
a small bonus.

Caution: There is a danger in recognition.
Be very careful with recognition
so that the rewards do not become
the reason the employee strives to achieve.
Let the best reward be a feeling of pride in doing a job well.
In other words,
praise a lot more
than you award or compensate.

Monitor your employees actions
and provide feedback that is clear,
objective, and
focused on the behavior you observed.

––––––––––––––

Tell your employees
what you like about their actions.
Be specific.
Saying "You did a good job" is too broad.
It does not express to the employee
the behavior you are praising.
"I liked the way you handled the customer
when you said _____"
lets the employee know
specifically what you liked.
The behavior is more apt to be repeated.

––––––––––––––

Do you take action on poor performers?
Or ignore the situation,
hoping it will correct itself?

Here is the bad news:
It will not.

Here is more bad news:
Your good employees will lose respect for you
if you do not handle the problem.

Always speak to your employees in a calm voice.
Never discuss a negative situation if you are angry.
Compose yourself,
try to see the situation
from your employee's perspective,
and then talk to the employee.

———————

When an employee's behavior
is one that needs to be corrected,
deal with it immediately
so the behavior can be changed.

———————

Here's a basic outline to follow:

Plan what you will say before
meeting with the employee.

Think about how the employee is going to respond.

When you meet,
briefly describe the behavior you observed.

Ask the employee to explain her actions.

Let the employee do most of the talking,
you most of the listening.

(Continued next page)

(Continued)
From the employee's response,
you will know if the behavior was caused
by a misunderstanding (training issue) or
by a lack of desire (motivation issue). *

Reach an agreement of what the desired behavior should be.

Let the employee know
what you will do to help her improve.

Ask the employee what she can do differently in the future.

Ask the employee to restate what the desired behavior is
and what will be done to get her there.

Affirm to her you know she can do it.

A note on training issue vs. motivation issue:
the responsibility of a training issue will fall on you
to see the employee receives the proper training;
the responsibility of a motivation issue
will be up to the employee to change her attitude.

Motivating To Develop High Performers
~ *Thoughts & Ideas* ~

Motivating To Develop High Performers

I motivate my employees by:

I will improve my motivational skills by:

Chapter 11

Conclusion

Finally, be the person you want your employees to be like. Never relax.

Be your best at all times. It is imperative to the success of your team.

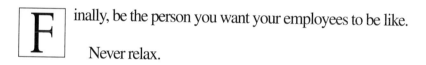

Conclusion
~ *Thoughts & Ideas* ~

Conclusion

The most valuable lesson I learned about myself after reading this book is: